Quantum Quips

Bob Seeman

ISBN: 9798371376756 (Hardcover)
ISBN: 9798371375834 (Paperback)

Cover design by: CyberCurb

Publisher: CyberCurb, Vancouver

About the Author

Bob Seeman is a Director of the Cyber Future Foundation Canada, an international collaboration of industry, public agencies and academia to build a more trusted and secure internet. Bob is the Managing Partner of CyberCurb and advises government and business internationally on technology, legal and business issues.

Bob has also published *On Trust, How Business Decisions Really Get Made, Power in Mistake, Artificial Intelligentsia,* and the foremost bitcoin-skeptic book, *The Coinmen.*

He is a California attorney, electrical engineer, and board director. Bob is a co-founder and former director of RIWI Corp., a public company that conducts data analytics. Previously, he was Head of Strategy for Microsoft Network in London, and a technical consultant to the European Commission.

Bob previously practiced administrative law with an international law firm. He holds a Bachelor of Applied Science (Elec. Eng.) with Honours from the University of Toronto, a Master of Business Administration from EDHEC, and a Juris Doctor (J.D.) from the University of British Columbia.

For Rosie.

Table of Contents

Max Planck

German theoretical physicist, 1858 – 1947

"The Theory of Relativity confers an absolute meaning on a magnitude which in classical theory has only a relative significance: the velocity of light. The velocity of light is to the Theory of Relativity as the elementary quantum of action is to the Quantum Theory: it is its absolute core."

Max Planck, the physicist who originated quantum theory, was a talented pianist. At one point, he considered becoming a professional pianist. He played throughout his life. His piano playing was his one constant.

Albert Einstein

Theoretical physicist, 1879 – 1955

"While the finish given to our picture of the world by the theory of relativity has already been absorbed into the general scientific consciousness, this has scarcely occurred to the same extent with those aspects of the general problem of knowledge which have been elucidated by the quantum theory."

"I cannot seriously believe in [quantum theory] because the theory cannot be reconciled with the idea that physics should represent a reality in time and space, free from spooky actions at a distance."

"[I can't accept quantum mechanics because] "I like to think the moon is there even if I am not looking at it."

"The mathematical framework of quantum theory has passed countless successful tests and is now universally accepted as a consistent and accurate description of all atomic phenomena."

"The more success the quantum theory has, the sillier it looks"

"Quantum physics thus reveals a basic oneness of the universe."

"Everything we call real is made of things that cannot be regarded as real."

"When asked… [about] an underlying quantum world, Bohr would answer, 'There is no quantum world. There is only an abstract quantum physical description. It is wrong to think that the task of physics is to find out how nature is. Physics concerns what we can say about Nature.'"

"As far as the laws of mathematics refer to reality, they are not certain, and as far as they are certain, they do not refer to reality."

"Quantum mechanics is certainly imposing. But an inner voice tells me that this is not yet the real thing. The theory says a lot, but does not bring us any closer to the secrets of the 'Old One.' I, at any rate, am convinced that He is not playing at dice."

"Only two things are infinite, the universe and human stupidity, and I'm not sure about the former."

Albert Einstein, the famous physicist and mathematician, had poor grades in school and was thought to have a learning disability. Later in life, when asked a difficult question, he replied, "Who do you think I am? Einstein?"

Niels Bohr

Danish physicist, 1885 – 1962

"It is wrong to think that the task of physics is to find out how nature is. Physics concerns what we say about nature."

"We must be clear that when it comes to atoms, language can be used only as in poetry."

"Those who are not shocked when they first come across quantum theory cannot possibly have understood it."

Niels Bohr helped us understand atomic structure and quantum mechanics. He was a competitive soccer player and an enthusiastic supporter of the Danish national team. He had a soccer ball hanging in his office at the Institute for Theoretical Physics in Copenhagen. Is it just a coincidence that the atomic structure (opposite) is vaguely reminiscent of a soccer ball?

Erwin Schrödinger

Austrian physicist, 1887 – 1961

"The mathematical framework of quantum theory has passed countless successful tests and is now universally accepted as a consistent and accurate description of all atomic phenomena."

"The verbal interpretation, on the other hand, i.e. the metaphysics of quantum physics, is on far less solid ground. In fact, in more than forty years physicists have not been able to provide a clear metaphysical model."

"I do not like it, and I am sorry I ever had anything to do with it."

Erwin Schrödinger, best known for his Schrödinger equation below, was an accomplished mountaineer and enjoyed hiking in the Alps. He also had a passion for philosophy and was interested in the concepts of identity and reality. He did not like cats.

$$H(t) \, | \, \psi(t) \rangle = i\hbar \frac{d}{dt} \, | \, \psi(t) \rangle$$

Albert Szent-Gyorgyi

Hungarian biochemist, 1893 – 1986

"Nature is one. It is not divided into physics, chemistry, quantum mechanics."

Albert Szent-Gyorgyi received the Nobel Prize in Physiology or Medicine in 1937. He was an avid collector of oriental rugs and had a large collection in his laboratory, many with chemical stains. He was also a committed peace activist and was involved in various peace organizations throughout his life.

Werner Heisenberg

German theoretical physicist, 1901 – 1976

"The uncertainty principle refers to the degree of indeterminateness in the possible present knowledge of the simultaneous values of various quantities with which the quantum theory deals; it does not restrict, for example, the exactness of a position measurement alone or a velocity measurement alone."

"[T]he atoms or elementary particles themselves are not real; they form a world of potentialities or possibilities rather than one of things or facts."

"It is true that in quantum theory we cannot rely on strict causality. But by repeating the experiments many times, we can finally derive from the observations statistical distributions, and by repeating such series of experiments, we can arrive at objective statements concerning these distributions."

"After the conversations about Indian philosophy, some of the ideas of Quantum Physics that had seemed so crazy suddenly made much more sense."

"Not only is the Universe stranger than we think, it is stranger than we can think."

Werner Heisenberg is known for his uncertainty principle. However, he knew what he was doing. He was a skilled pianist and had a strong appreciation for music. He often played chamber music with other physicists and musicians, and considered music to be a source of inspiration for his scientific work. Music and physics seems to go together. Perhaps physics is the music of life?

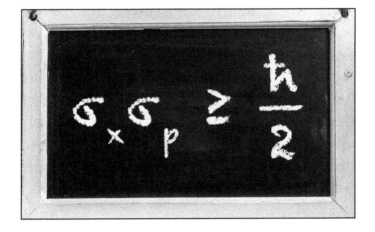

Pascual Jordan

German theoretical and mathematical
physicist, 1902 – 1980

"Observations not only disturb what is to be
measured, they produce it."

Pascual Jordan, a top quantum mechanics
and quantum field theory physicist, was a
committed pacifist and anti-war activist. He
was imprisoned for his beliefs during World
War II and was a member of the German
resistance movement. After the war, he
was a founding member of the Socialist
German Student League and was actively
involved in promoting peace and
disarmament. Sadly, he died before the
Berlin Wall came down.

Eugene Wigner

Hungarian-American theoretical physicist, 1902 – 1995

"When the province of physical theory was extended to encompass microscopic phenomena through the creation of quantum mechanics, the concept of consciousness came to the fore again. It was not possible to formulate the laws of quantum mechanics in a fully consistent way without reference to the consciousness."

Eugene Wigner's work was focussed on quantum mechanics, nuclear physics, and the theory of symmetry in physical systems. He was a member of the Budapest String Quartet for many years and considered pursuing a career in music before deciding to study physics. Wigner believed that the mathematical beauty he found in physics was similar to the beauty he found in music. Physics, the essence of life itself, is beautiful.

Richard Feynman

American theoretical physicist, 1918 – 1988

"I think I can safely say that nobody understands Quantum Mechanics."

"The rule of simulation that I would like to have is that the number of computer elements required to simulate a large physical system is only to be proportional to the space-time volume of the physical system."

"Now I explicitly go to the question of how we can simulate with a computer... the quantum mechanical effects... But the full description of quantum mechanics for a large system with R particles... cannot be simulated with a normal computer."

"Can you do it with a new kind of computer – a quantum computer? Now it turns out, as far as I can tell, that you can simulate this with a quantum system, with quantum computer elements. It's not a Turing machine, but a machine of a different kind."

"You know how it always is, every new idea, it takes a generation or two until it becomes obvious that there's no real problem. It has not yet become obvious to me that there's no real problem. I cannot define the real problem, therefore I suspect there's no real problem, but I'm not sure there's no real problem."

"The chance is high that the truth lies in the fashionable direction. But, on the off-chance that it is in another direction – a direction obvious from an unfashionable view of field theory – who will find it? Only someone who has sacrificed himself by teaching himself quantum electrodynamics from a peculiar and unusual point of view; one that he may have to invent for himself."

"The 'paradox' is only a conflict between reality and your feeling of what reality 'ought to be.' "

"A philosopher once said, 'It is necessary for the very existence of science that the same conditions always produce the same results.' Well, they don't!"

"It is a curious historical fact that modern quantum mechanics began with two quite different mathematical formulations: the differential equation of Schroedinger and the matrix algebra of Heisenberg. The two apparently dissimilar approaches were proved to be mathematically equivalent."

"Because the theory of quantum mechanics could explain all of chemistry and the various properties of substances, it was a tremendous success. But still there was the problem of the interaction of light and matter."

"With the exception of gravitation and radioactivity, all of the phenomena known to physicists and chemists in 1911 have their ultimate explanation in the laws of quantum electrodynamics."

"The extreme weakness of quantum gravitational effects now poses some philosophical problems; maybe nature is trying to tell us something new here: maybe we should not try to quantize gravity."

"Trying to understand the way nature works involves a most terrible test of human reasoning ability. It involves subtle trickery, beautiful tightropes of logic on which one has to walk in order not to make a mistake in predicting what will happen. The quantum mechanical and the relativity ideas are examples of this."

"I present that as another interesting problem: To work out the classes of different kinds of quantum mechanical systems which are really intersimulatable – which are equivalent – as has been done in the case of classical computers."

Richard Feynman, a physicist who developed quantum mechanics and quantum electrodynamics, was a talented drummer and played in a swing band while he was a student at Princeton University. He was also an enthusiastic bongo player.

David Bohm

American-Brazilian-British scientist, 1917 –
1992

"In relativity, movement is continuous, causally
determinate and well defined, while in quantum
mechanics it is discontinuous, not causally
determinate and not well defined."

David Bohm's work on quantum mechanics challenged the prevailing interpretation. He proposed a new, holistic understanding of the quantum world. He developed a theory of "implicate order" to explain how the quantum and classical worlds are interconnected. He was a pacifist and a conscientious objector during World War II. He refused to participate in the development of the atomic bomb and went to jail instead. Bohm did not believe in the bomb.

James Lovelock

Scientist, 1919 – 2022

"If you start any large theory, such as quantum mechanics, plate tectonics, evolution, it takes about 40 years for mainstream science to come around. Gaia has been going for only 30 years or so."

James Lovelock developed the Gaia theory, which proposes that the Earth functions as a single self-regulating organism. He was a keen amateur inventor and had a passion for technology. James Lovelock was a self-taught scientist and he was not formally trained in any particular field of science. He built his first electronic device at the age of 10 and continued to work on various inventions throughout his life, including developing instruments for monitoring atmospheric gases. He invented the electron capture detector, a device used to measure trace levels of pollutants in the environment. With the development of both the Gaia theory and the pollution detector, Lovelock became one of the first environmentalists.

David Finkelstein

Professor of physics, 1929 – 2016

"Quantum theory was split up into dialects. Different people describe the same experiences in remarkably different languages. This is confusing even to physicists."

David Finkelstein was one of the pioneers of the study of black holes. Throughout his career, Finkelstein was interested in the intersection of physics and philosophy and the implications of his scientific work for our understanding of the world. He is also an accomplished musician and wrote and recorded several albums. However, despite spending decades of his life working on music, few listened to it – perhaps helping him understand the concept of the black hole.

Bernard d'Espagnat

French theoretical physicist, 1921 – 2015

"The doctrine that the world is made up of objects whose existence is independent of human consciousness turns out to be in conflict with quantum mechanics and with facts established by experiment."

Bernard d'Espagnat considered the relationship between science and spirituality.

Murray Gell-Mann

American physicist, 1929 – 2019

"If we look at the way the universe behaves, quantum mechanics gives us fundamental, unavoidable indeterminacy, so that alternative histories of the universe can be assigned probability."

Murray Gell-Mann was awarded the Nobel Prize in Physics in 1969 for the theory of the strong interaction, which governs the behavior of subatomic particles. He proposed the concept of "quarks", which became a central part of the standard model of particle physics.

Hugh Everett III

American physicist, 1930 – 1982

"[The Many-worlds interpretation is the] only completely coherent approach to explaining both the contents of quantum mechanics and the appearance of the world."

Hugh Everett III formulated the "many-worlds interpretation" of quantum mechanics. This theory proposes that every quantum event leads to the creation of multiple, parallel universes, each with its own unique set of properties. Everett's idea was initially considered controversial but has since become a widely discussed interpretation of quantum mechanics. People no longer think of Everett as being on another planet.

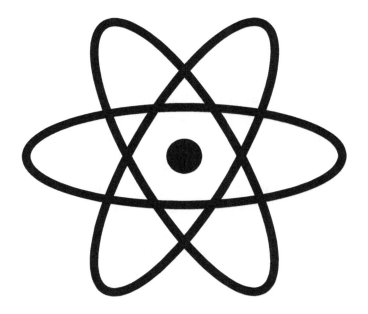

John Polkinghorne

English theoretical physicist, 1930 – 2021

"Quantum theory also tells us that the world is not simply objective; somehow it's something more subtle than that. In some sense it is veiled from us, but it has a structure that we can understand."

John Polkinghorne was a professor of mathematical physics at the University of Cambridge before leaving academia to study theology and becoming an ordained priest. Polkinghorne was a prominent voice in the dialogue between science and religion, arguing that the two can complement each other and provide a deeper understanding of the world.

Michael Crichton

American Author, 1942 – 2008

"Quantum technology turns ordinary reality upside down."

Michael Crichton was the author of many best-selling books, including *Jurassic Park*, *The Andromeda Strain*, and *Sphere*. He was known for his meticulous research and his ability to make complex scientific concepts accessible to a broad audience. Crichton was a trained physician and taught at Harvard Medical School.

Bob Seeman

Stephen Hawking

English theoretical physicist, cosmologist, and author, 1942 – 2018

"Quantum physics tells us that no matter how thorough our observation of the present, the (unobserved) past, like the future, is indefinite and exists only as a spectrum of possibilities.

"The universe, according to quantum physics, has no single past, or history. The fact that the past takes no definite form means that observations you make on a system in the present affect its past."

"To apply quantum theory to the entire universe... is tricky... particles of matter fired at a screen with two slits in it... exhibit interference patterns just as water waves do. Feynman showed that this arises because a particle does not have a unique history. That is, as it moves from its starting point A to some endpoint B, it doesn't take one definite path, but rather simultaneously takes every possible path connecting the two points. From this point of view, interference is no surprise because, for instance, the particle can travel through both slits at the same time and interfere with itself. In this view, the universe appeared spontaneously, starting off in every possible way."

"We are the product of quantum fluctuations in the very early universe."

"The Planck satellite may detect the imprint of the gravitational waves predicted by inflation. This would be quantum gravity written across the sky."

36

Despite being diagnosed with motor neuron disease at the age of 21 and given only a few years to live, Hawking went on to have a long and productive career. He wrote several influential books, including *A Brief History of Time*, which became a best-seller and popularized science for a general audience. He was known for his wit and humor.

There once was a genius called Hawking
Who couldn't do walking or talking
His body disabled
His mind multi-fabled
His brain power awesome and shocking.

Steven Weinberg

American theoretical physicist, 1933 – 2021

"When you do calculations using quantum mechanics, even when you are calculating something perfectly sensible like the energy of an atomic state, you get an answer that is infinite. This means you are wrong - but how do you deal with that? Is there something wrong with the theory, or something wrong with the way you are doing the calculation?

Steven Weinberg was awarded the Nobel Prize in Physics in 1979 for the unification of the weak and electromagnetic forces. He was also a noted public intellectual and wrote extensively on the relationship between science and religion, the role of science in society, and the public understanding of science.

Fritjof Capra

Austrian-born American physicist

"Quantum theory thus reveals a basic oneness of the universe. It shows that we cannot decompose the world into independently existing smallest units. As we penetrate into matter, nature does not show us any isolated "building blocks," but rather appears as a complicated web of relations between the various parts of the whole. These relations always include the observer in an essential way. The human observer constitute the final link in the chain of observational processes, and the properties of any atomic object can be understood only in terms of the object's interaction with the observer."

Fritjof Capra is the author of several influential books, including *The Tao of Physics*, which explores the connection between modern physics and Eastern mysticism, and *The Web of Life*, which presents a systems view of life and ecology.

Lawrence Krauss

American theoretical physicist and cosmologist

"At the heart of quantum mechanics is a rule that sometimes governs politicians or CEOs – as long as no one is watching, anything goes."

"No one intuitively understands quantum mechanics because all of our experience involves a world of classical phenomena where, for example, a baseball thrown from pitcher to catcher seems to take just one path, the one described by Newton's laws of motion. Yet at a microscopic level, the universe behaves quite differently."

"For the record: Quantum mechanics does not deny the existence of objective reality. Nor does it imply that mere thoughts can change external events. Effects still require causes, so if you want to change the universe, you need to act on it."

"Feynman once said, 'Science is imagination in a straitjacket.' It is ironic that in the case of quantum mechanics, the people without the straitjackets are generally the nuts."

Lawrence Krauss is known for his work in the fields of dark matter and dark energy, as well as his contributions to the popular understanding of science. He is the author of several books, including *The Physics of the Impossible* and *A Universe from Nothing*, in which he explores the latest scientific understanding of the origins and evolution of the universe.

> The bell curve is called after Gauss
> Just like waltzes are named after Strauss
> He's incurred lots of wrath
> But in physics and math
> The name to remember is Krauss.

Wolfgang Ketterle

German Professor of physics

"Amplifying atoms is more subtle than amplifying electromagnetic waves because atoms can only change their quantum state and cannot be created. Therefore, even if one could amplify gold atoms, one would not realize the dreams of medieval alchemy."

Wolfgang Ketterle was awarded the Nobel Prize in Physics in 2001. He was one of the pioneers in the field of ultra-cold atomic gases, and his work has led to a deeper understanding of the behavior of these systems and their potential applications in fields such as quantum computing and precision sensing.

Roger Penrose

English mathematician, mathematical physicist, philosopher of science

"Quantum mechanics makes absolutely no sense."

Roger Penrose, awarded the Nobel Prize in Physics in 2020, is known for his work on singularities and the nature of the universe. He has written several books, including *The Emperor's New Mind* and *Shadows of the Mind*, in which he explores the relationship between mathematics, physics, and consciousness.

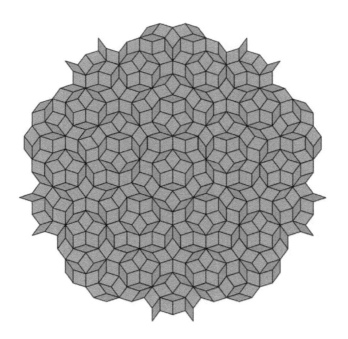

Christophe Galfard

French physicist and writer

"When left alone, quantum particles behave as multiple images of themselves (as waves, really), simultaneously moving through all possible paths in space and time. Now, again, why do we not experience this multitude around ourselves? Is it because we are probing things around us all the time? Why do all experiments that involve, say, the position of a particle make the particle suddenly be somewhere rather than everywhere? No one knows. Before you probe it, a particle is a wave of possibilities. After you've probed it, it is somewhere, and subsequently it is somewhere for ever, rather than everywhere again. Strange, that. Nothing, within the laws of quantum physics, allows for such a collapse to happen. It is an experimental mystery and a theoretical one. Quantum physics stipulates that whenever something is there, it can transform into something else, of course, but it cannot disappear. And since quantum physics allows for multiple possibilities simultaneously, these possibilities should then keep existing, even after a measurement is made. But they don't. Every possibility but one vanishes. We do not see any of the others around us. We live in a classical world, where everything is based on quantum laws but nothing resembles the quantum world."

"The very small quantum world, it seems, is a mixture of possibilities. The quantum fields to which all particles belong are the sum of these possibilities and, somehow, one possibility is chosen out of all the existing ones just by seeing it, just by the very act of detecting it, whenever one tries to probe a particle's nature. Nobody knows why or how this happens."

"The air around you is filled with floating atoms, sliding down the Earth's spacetime curve. Atoms first assembled in the cores of long-dead stars. Atoms within you, everywhere, disintegrating in radioactive decays. Beneath your feet, the floor – whose electrons refuse to let yours pass, thus making you able to stand and walk and run. Earth, your planet, a lump of matter made out of the three quantum fields known to mankind, held together by gravity, the so-called fourth force (even though it isn't a force), floating within and through spacetime."

Christophe Galfard makes complex scientific concepts accessible to a wider audience.

Sten F. Odenwald

Swedish-American astronomer, author

"Quantum fluctuations are, at their root, completely acausal, in the sense that cause and effect and ordering of events in time is not a part of how these fluctuations work. Because of this, there seem not to be any correlations built into these kinds of fluctuations because 'law' as we understand the term requires some kind of cause-and-effect structure to pre-exist. Quantum fluctuations can precede physical law, but it seems that the converse is not true. So in the big bang, the establishment of 'law' came after the event itself, but of course even the concept of time and causality may not have been quite the same back then as they are now."

Sten F. Odenwald has helped the popular understanding of astronomy and space science. He is the author of several books, including *The Cambridge Guide to the Solar System*.

Neil Turok

South African physicist

"Quantum physics is one of the hardest things to understand intuitively, because essentially the whole point is that our classical picture is wrong."

"Quantum physics forms the foundation of chemistry, explaining how molecules are held together. It describes how real solids and materials behave and how electricity is conducted through them.... It enabled the development of transistors, integrated circuits, lasers, LEDs, digital cameras and all the modern gadgetry that surrounds us."

Neil Turok's research has focused on the early universe, inflation, the cosmic microwave background, and the nature of dark matter and dark energy. He is not funded with dark money.

Richard Morgan

British science fiction and fantasy author

"In the future, maybe quantum mechanics will teach us something equally chilling about exactly how we exist from moment to moment of what we like to think of as time."

Richard K. Morgan is best known for his *Altered Carbon* series, which is set in a future world where people's consciousness can be stored on a disk and transferred from one body to another – the ultimate out-of-body experience.

Alan Guth

American theoretical physicist and cosmologist

"It is rather fantastic to realize that the laws of physics can describe how everything was created in a random quantum fluctuation out of nothing, and how over the course of 15 billion years, matter could organize in such complex ways that we have human beings sitting here, talking, doing things intentionally."

Alan Guth proposed and developed the idea of cosmic inflation, making it one of the most widely accepted explanations for the large-scale structure of the universe.

Frank Tipler

American mathematical physicist and cosmologist

"What you can show using physics, forces this universe to continue to exist. As long as you're using general relativity and quantum mechanics you are forced to conclude that God exists."

Frank J. Tipler developed a controversial theory known as the "Omega Point," which argues that the ultimate fate of the universe is a single, ultimate point of infinite density and complexity that represents the end of time. Despite this theory, Tipler is an optimist.

Francis Collins

American physician-geneticist

"I became an atheist because, as a graduate student studying quantum physics, life seemed to be reducible to second-order differential equations. Mathematics, chemistry and physics had it all. And I didn't see any need to go beyond that."

"I finished up my graduate degree in quantum mechanics, but underwent a bit of a personal crisis, recognizing that I didn't want to do that for the rest of my life. It was too abstract, too far removed from human concerns."

Francis Collins led the Human Genome Project, a massive international effort to map and sequence the entire human genome. He is also a prominent advocate for the integration of science and spirituality, and has written several books on the subject, including the best-seller *The Language of God: A Scientist Presents Evidence for Belief.*

Yuan T. Lee

Taiwanese Professor of chemistry

"Because of recent improvements in the accuracy of theoretical predictions based on large scale ab initio quantum mechanical calculations, meaningful comparisons between theoretical and experimental findings have become possible."

"In fact any experiment that measures a quantum effect is one in which the quantum effect is aligned with the behavior of some heavy, macroscopic object; that's how we measure it."

"The chaos can act as a magnifier of quantum fluctuations so that they can produce sizable effects in the world around us. But we know that that can happen often."

"If we look at the way the universe behaves, quantum mechanics gives us fundamental, unavoidable indeterminacy, so that alternative histories of the universe can be assigned probability."

Yuan T. Lee was awarded the Nobel Prize in Chemistry in 1986 for his work in the field of chemical dynamics. Lee's research has helped to advance our understanding of chemical reactions and how they occur at the molecular level. He is best known for his development of the technique of Fourier Transform Ion Cyclotron

Resonance (FTICR) mass spectrometry, which allows for the precise measurement of the mass of individual molecules in a sample.

Alain Aspect

French physicist

"The main ingredient of the first quantum revolution, wave-particle duality, has led to inventions such as the transistor and the laser that are at the root of the information society."

Alain Aspect pioneered experiments on the phenomenon of quantum entanglement, in which two or more particles can become correlated in such a way that the state of one particle can instantaneously affect the state of the other, regardless of the distance between them. These experiments demonstrated that quantum mechanics is a non-local theory, meaning that particles can be connected in ways that cannot be explained by classical physics.

Aspect is a trained classical violinist and has a strong interest in music. In fact, he has been known to play the violin in his laboratory in order to calm himself down and help him focus when working on difficult problems. He has also been known to combine his interests in physics and music by giving lectures on the physics of music and the connections between the two fields. Aspect presents different aspects.

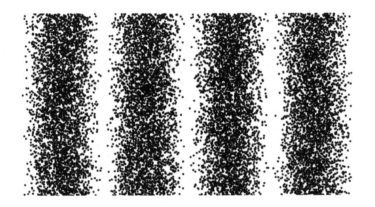

Adam Riess

American Professor of astrophysics

"One of the most exciting things about dark energy is that it seems to live at the very nexus of two of our most successful theories of physics: quantum mechanics, which explains the physics of the small, and Einstein's Theory of General Relativity, which explains the physics of the large, including gravity."

Adam Riess was awarded the Nobel Prize in Physics in 2011 for his work on the discovery of the accelerating expansion of the universe. Riess' research showed that the universe is expanding at an ever-increasing rate, driven by a mysterious force that has come to be known as dark energy. This discovery challenged the prevailing understanding of the universe and has since become one of the most important and widely studied areas of astrophysics.

David Deutsch

British physicist

"Quantum computation is... nothing less than a distinctly new way of harnessing nature ... It will be the first technology that allows useful tasks to be performed in collaboration between parallel universes, and then sharing the results."

"The most important application of quantum computing in the future is likely to be a computer simulation of quantum systems, because that's an application where we know for sure that quantum systems in general cannot be efficiently simulated on a classical computer."

"To me quantum computation is a new and deeper and better way to understand the laws of physics, and hence understanding physical reality as a whole."

David Deutsch has helped us understand the foundations of quantum mechanics and the nature of knowledge, reality, and the limits of science.

Julian Baggini

Philosopher, journalist and author

"Science works because the phenomenon being described can be relied on to remain the same. Even in quantum physics, where phenomena are changed by observation, the way in which observation interferes is regular and falls within a limited range of possibilities. Human culture, however, has the nasty habit of never staying the same for very long."

Julian Baggini is a British philosopher, author, and co-founder of *The Philosophers' Magazine*. He has written several books on philosophy, including *The Ethics Toolkit* and *The Ego Trick*. Baggini is also known for his writings on practical ethics, the relationship between science and philosophy, and the philosophy of food.

Brian Greene

American theoretical physicist,
mathematician, and string theorist

"Einstein's theory of relativity does a fantastic job for explaining big things. Quantum mechanics is fantastic for the other end of the spectrum – for small things."

"Quantum mechanics broke the mold of the previous framework, classical mechanics, by establishing that the predictions of science are necessarily probabilistic."

Brian Greene is a well-known physicist and author who popularizes science to a general audience. He is an accomplished saxophonist and has played in jazz clubs and jam sessions.

Kip Thorne

American theoretical physicist

"We have to have a combination of general relativity that describes the warping of space and time, and quantum physics, which describes the uncertainties in that warping and how they change."

"In subjects that physicists think of as purely quantum, classical ideas and classical computational techniques can often be powerful."

Kip Thorne has helped us to understand black holes and gravitational waves. He was a science advisor for the film *Interstellar*, ensuring the scientific accuracy of the film's depictions of black holes and wormholes.

David Gross

American theoretical physicist and string theorist

"When I was at Berkeley, the framework of quantum field theory could calculate the dynamics of electromagnetism. It could roughly describe the motion of the weak nuclear force, radiation. But it hit a brick wall with the strong interaction, the binding force."

"I had set out to disprove quantum field theory – and the opposite occurred! I was shocked."

David Gross is a founding member of the "Eightfold Way" particle classification scheme, which led to the discovery of the quark structure of matter.

Leonard Susskind

American professor of theoretical physics

"You have to say now that space is something. Space can vibrate, space can fluctuate, space can be quantum mechanical, but what the devil is it?"

"The most important single thing about string theory is that it's a highly mathematical theory, and the mathematics holds together in a very tight and consistent way. It contains in its basic structure both quantum mechanics and the theory of gravity. That's big news."

Leonard Susskind was initially trained as an electrical engineer and worked in industry before becoming a physicist. Only later did he work in the field of theoretical physics, particularly in the areas of string theory and quantum field theory.

Bob Seeman

Martin Rees

British cosmologist and astrophysicist

"In the beginning there were only probabilities. The universe could only come into existence if someone observed it. It does not matter that the observers turned up several billion years later. The universe exists because we are aware of it."

"Before the discovery of quantum mechanics, the framework of physics was this: If you tell me how things are now, I can then use the laws of physics to calculate, and hence predict, how things will be later."

"String theory is the most developed theory with the capacity to unite general relativity and quantum mechanics in a consistent manner. I do believe the universe is consistent, and therefore I do believe that general relativity and quantum mechanics should be put together in a manner that makes sense."

"It is astonishing that human brains, which evolved to cope with the everyday world, have been able to grasp the counterintuitive mysteries of the cosmos and the quantum."

"Everything, however complicated – breaking waves, migrating birds, and tropical forests – is made of atoms and obeys the equations of quantum physics. But even if those equations could be solved, they wouldn't offer the enlightenment that scientists seek. Each science has its own autonomous concepts and laws."

"Indeed, our everyday world presents intellectual challenges just as daunting as those of the cosmos and the quantum, and that is where 99 per cent of scientists focus their efforts. Even the smallest insect, with its intricate structure, is far more complex than either an atom or a star."

Martin Rees is a member of the British House of Lords, using his position to advocate for science and technology policy. Rees is a prolific author and has written several books on cosmology, science and public policy, including *Just Six Numbers*, *Our Final Hour*, and *Before the Beginning*.

Michio Kaku

American theoretical physicist, futurist, and popularizer of science

"It is often stated that of all the theories proposed in this century, the silliest is quantum theory. In fact, some say that the only thing that quantum theory has going for it is that it is unquestionably correct."

"If we do get a quantum theory of spacetime, it should answer some of the deepest philosophical questions that we have, like what happened before the big bang?

"When you look at the calculation, it's amazing that every time you try to prove or disprove time travel, you've pushed Einstein's theory to the very limits where quantum effects must dominate. That's telling us that you really need a theory of everything to resolve this question. And the only candidate is string theory."

Michio Kaku, a theoretical physicist and popular science writer, is known for his work on string theory.

Ashoke Sen

Indian Professor of theoretical physicist

"In many ways, string theory attempts to go beyond Einstein's dream... an all-encompassing description of nature that works at large distances where gravity becomes important as well as small distances where quantum mechanics is important."

Ashoke Sen has been instrumental in developing the concept of "duality" in string theory, which connects seemingly different physical phenomena into a single unifying framework.

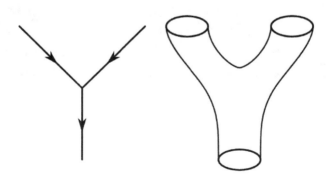

Lee Smolin

American theoretical physicist

"Every string theory that's been written down says the speed of light is universal. But other ideas about quantum gravity predict the speed of light has actually increased."

Lee Smolin is an advocate for the idea that our universe is one of many in a multiverse. He has also written several popular science books, including *The Life of the Cosmos* and *Time Reborn.*

Edward Witten

American mathematical and theoretical physicist

"Quantum mechanics brought an unexpected fuzziness into physics because of quantum uncertainty, the Heisenberg uncertainty principle. String theory does so again because a point particle is replaced by a string, which is more spread out."

Edward Witten is a mathematical physicist who was once a chess prodigy and won several chess tournaments as a child.

Jungsang Kim

Quantum researcher

"Back in the 1940s, researchers were just discovering how to use vacuum tubes as simple switches. ... These switches could then form logic gates, which could be linked together to form the first logic circuits. That's where we're at now with quantum processors. We have verified that all the components work. The next step is to engineer the smallest, yet most interesting circuit possible."

Jungsang Kim is best known for his work on the experimental demonstration of quantum teleportation and quantum cloning.

Philip Ball

British science writer

"Computer simulation often works fine if we assume nothing more than Newton's laws at the atomic scale, even though we know that really we should be using quantum, not classical, mechanics at that level. But sometimes approximating the behaviour of atoms as though they were classical billiard-ball particles isn't sufficient. We really do need to take quantum behaviour into account to accurately model chemical reactions involved in industrial catalysis or drug action, say. We can do that by solving the Schrödinger equation for the particles, but only approximately: we need to make lots of simplifications if the maths is to be tractable. But what if we had a computer that itself works by the laws of quantum mechanics? Then the sort of behaviour you're trying to simulate is built into the very way the machine operates: it is hardwired into the fabric. This was the point Feynman made in his article. But no such machines existed. At any rate they would, as he pointed out with wry understatement, be 'machines of a different kind' from any computer built so far. Feynman didn't work out the full theory of what such a machine would look like or how it would work – but he insisted that 'if you want to make a simulation of nature, you'd better make it quantum-mechanical'."

Philip Ball has written numerous books and articles on a wide range of scientific subjects, including physics, chemistry, materials science, and the history of science. He is a trained chemist and has a PhD in the physical chemistry of materials. Before becoming a science writer, he worked as a researcher in the field of materials science, specifically in the study of complex fluids and colloids.

Seth Lloyd

Professor of mechanical engineering

"Programmed by quanta, physics gave rise first to chemistry and then to life; programmed by mutations and recombination, life gave rise to Shakespeare; programmed by experience and imagination, Shakespeare gave rise to Hamlet."

"Quantum mechanics is weird. I don't understand it. Just live with it. You don't have to understand the nature of things in order to build cool devices."

"If you wanted to build the most powerful computer you could, you can't do better than including everything in the universe that's potentially available."

"A classical computation is like a solo voice – one line of pure tones succeeding each other. A quantum computation is like a symphony – many lines of tones interfering with one another."

"We couldn't build quantum computers unless the universe were quantum and computing. We can build such machines because the universe is storing and processing information in the quantum realm. When we build quantum computers, we're hijacking that underlying computation in order to make it do things we want: little and/or/not calculations. We're hacking into the universe."

"The history of the universe is, in effect, a huge and ongoing quantum computation. The universe is a quantum computer."

"In order to figure out how to make atoms compute, you have to learn how to speak their language and to understand how they process information under normal circumstances."

"When you zap things with light to build quantum computers, you're hacking existing systems. You're hijacking the computation that's already happening in the universe, just like a hacker takes over someone else's computer."

"[With quantum computers] you can calculate how many bits are in the universe, how much energy it takes to flip them, how much energy exists, and use that to rule out lots of things about the universe's history. Anything that takes more bit flips couldn't have happened."

"The primary consequence of the computational nature of the universe is that the universe naturally generates complex systems, such as life. Although the basic laws of physics are comparatively simple in form, they give rise, because they are computationally universal, to systems of enormous complexity."

"At some point, Moore's law will break down."

"Science has an uncomfortable way of pushing human beings from center stage. In our prescientific stories, humans began as the focal point of Nature, living on an Earth that was the center of the universe. As the origins of the Earth and of mankind were investigated more carefully, it became clear that Nature had other interests beyond people, and the Earth was less central than previously hoped. Humankind was just one branch of the great family of life, and the Earth is a smallish planet orbiting an unexceptional sun quite far out on one arm of a run-of-the-mill spiral galaxy."

"Quantum mechanics is just completely strange and counterintuitive. We can't believe that things can be here [in one place] and there [in another place] at the same time. And yet that's a fundamental piece of quantum mechanics. So then the question is, life is dealing us weird lemons, can we make some weird lemonade from this?

"Yes, I am a quantum mechanic! Those darn quantum computers break all the time."

"All physical systems can be thought of as registering and processing information, and how one wishes to define computation will determine your view of what computation consists of."

"Every physical system registers information, and just by evolving in time, by doing its thing, it changes that information, transforms that information, or, if you like, processes that information."

"What's happened with society is that we have created these devices, computers, which already can register and process huge amounts of information, which is a significant fraction of the amount of information that human beings themselves, as a species, can process."

"Of course, one way of thinking about all of life and civilization is as being about how the world registers and processes information. Certainly that's what sex is about; that's what history is about."

"For hundreds of millions of years, Sex was the most efficient method for propagating information of dubious provenance: the origins of all those snippets of junk DNA are lost in the sands of reproductive history. Move aside, Sex: the world-wide Web has usurped your role."

"By separating the function of adaptation from the function of maintaining the integrity of individual genes, sex allows much greater diversity while still keeping genes whole. Sex is not only fun, it is good engineering practice."

"The amount of information that can be stored by the ultimate laptop, 10 to the 31st bits, is much higher than the 10 to the 10th bits stored on current laptops. ... Indeed, as the above calculation indicates, to take full advantage of the memory space available, the ultimate laptop must turn all its matter into energy."

"Some folks think life and technology and mind can keep expanding forever. Others say it can't. We are still not clear on that."

"Meaning is like pornography, you know it when you see it."

"Nothing in life is certain except death, taxes and the second law of thermodynamics. All three are processes in which useful or accessible forms of some quantity, such as energy or money, are transformed into useless, inaccessible forms of the same quantity. That is not to say that these three processes don't have fringe benefits: taxes pay for roads and schools; the second law of thermodynamics drives cars, computers and metabolism; and death, at the very least, opens up tenured faculty positions."

"I have not proved that the universe is, in fact, a digital computer and that it's capable of performing universal computation, but it's plausible that it is."

"If you take a more Darwinian point of view the dynamics of the universe are such that as the universe evolved in time, complex systems arose out of the natural dynamics of the universe."

"According to the standard model billions of years ago some little quantum fluctuation, perhaps a slightly lower density of matter, maybe right where we're sitting right now, caused our galaxy to start collapsing around here."

"Similarly, another famous little quantum fluctuation that programs you is the exact configuration of your DNA."

Seth Lloyd is a renowned quantum mechanical engineer and computer scientist. He is a former professional tango dancer, and he incorporates ideas from tango into his approach to physics and engineering. He has described tango as a way to illustrate complex mathematical and scientific concepts in a tangible way, and has used dance lessons to teach quantum mechanics to undergraduate students. As he might say, "Since it takes two to tango, it takes two to entangle."

Alex M. Vikoulov

Russian-American futurist

"With advanced quantum computational systems in place, we could have computed the COVID-19 vaccine within hours, if not minutes, of its discovery. Perhaps, any kind of life-threatening virus, since it is nothing more than a piece of code, will be completely preventable with the advances in quantum computing and computational biology. The question is, then, if we could eventually shield ourselves against the common viral micro-threat, what would a macro-threat of unknown nature mean for the human-machine civilization? We might soon need to decode another message from the transcendent realm edging us ever closer to the Cybernetic Singularity of some sort."

Alex M. Vikoulov is a Russian-American futurist, evolutionary cyberneticist, philosopher of mind, author and filmmaker.

Isaac Chuang

American electrical engineer and physicist

"We show that Shor's algorithm, the most complex quantum algorithm known to date, is realizable in a way where, yes, all you have to do is go in the lab, apply more technology, and you should be able to make a bigger quantum computer... . It might still cost an enormous amount of money to build – you won't be building a quantum computer and putting it on your desktop anytime soon – but now it's much more an engineering effort, and not a basic physics question."

Isaac Chuang co-authored the first book on quantum computing and has made significant contributions to the development of scalable quantum computing and quantum error correction.

Richard Dawkins

British evolutionary biologist and author

"There does seem to be a sense in which physics has gone beyond what human intuition can understand. We shouldn't be too surprised about that because we're evolved to understand things that move at a medium pace at a medium scale. We can't cope with the very tiny scale of quantum physics or the very large scale of relativity."

Richard Dawkins has published many books, including *The God Delusion* and several collections of poems such as *Biodiversity Heritage* and *The Fundamental Practices*.